I0180466

LEADERSHIP STYLES & LEVELS OF CHURCH

REVISED EDITION

GORDON MOORE

Ark House Press
PO Box 1722, Port Orchard, WA 98366 USA
PO Box 1321, Mona Vale NSW 1660 Australia
PO Box 318 334, West Harbour, Auckland 0661 New Zealand
arkhousepress.com

© 2015 Gordon Moore

All rights reserved. No part of this publication may be reproduced, stor
in a retrieval system or transmitted in any form or by any means electron
mechanical, photocopying, recording or otherwise without the prior writt
permission of the publisher.

Cataloguing in Publication Data:
Title: Leadership Styles & Levels of Church
ISBN: 9780994367556 (pbk.)
Subjects: Church growth/Leadership
Other Authors/Contributors: Moore, Gordon

Design and layout by initiateagency.com

CONTENTS

INTRODUCTION

Our generation is witnessing a church age of unprecedented conversions to Christ, yet small churches still seem to dominate the world church scene with an average size of 75 members. My experience and observations over the past thirty years have led me to two possible reasons for this.

Firstly, I believe that not enough Christians and Leaders are championing the Local Church as the centrepiece of God's work. There seems to be a lot of activity around the body of Christ, but no significant growth in the average size of the local church. Resources are often spread 'across the Body' but the bottom line is no resultant growth of the local churches.

Secondly, the church continues to function in the styles of leadership and ministry that are proving to be insufficient in producing growth and advancement of the local church.

It is this second reason that interests me as a local church practitioner and overseer. I believe that fresh ways need to be discovered on how to do church. Also, leaders need to be more effective in planting and growing the kind of churches that will make a greater impact on our unchurched communities.

My passion for the local church has prompted much consideration and subsequent discussions with my colleagues in C3 Church Global. This has led us to discover new approaches and styles of leadership that will help us break the prevailing culture of small churches that is proving to be insufficient in reaching our world.

One initiative that we have adopted in our movement of churches is to set the bar for churches at the world average of 75 members. In other words, if a 'church' cannot break this barrier of the 'primary group', they remain an 'outreach' or 'satellite' of a sponsoring church until they do. One pleasing result that has occurred is that most of our church plants break through this barrier in the first twelve months! When a shift in paradigm occurs, a shift in productivity follows.

Part of this journey has been my development of this 'Leadership Styles Model' that has proven helpful in providing leaders with a means to assess and develop their leadership skills as local church leaders. Because this model is new, quotations and references from other sources are limited. However, I believe this does not limit its application to the local church practitioner.

I trust the material presented in this book will help you grow and develop as a leader to enable you to take your church and ministry to new levels of effectiveness.

Gordon Moore Ph.D
Author

Chapter One

THE FOUR TEMPERAMENTS

Chapter One

There has been a healthy development of personality theories over recent years, such as by Florence Littauer, Tim LaHaye, Myers-Briggs, the DISC system and many others.

The study and application of the personality theories has been part of my journey over the last 30 years as a local church practitioner; a role that requires a high degree of people understanding and people skills.

Florence Littauer's work on Hippocrates' theory of the Four Temperaments has been most popular[1], and I have discovered it useful for describing Leadership Styles. For those readers who are not familiar with Littauer's personality profile system, Personality Plus, the following will give them an overview.

The Four Temperaments

The Phlegmatic Temperament – 'The Peacefuls'

The Phlegmatic motto is 'Let's do it the easy way'. This desire is basic to the Phlegmatic temperament. Their emotional needs include a sense of respect, feeling of worth, understanding, and emotional support. They have high interpersonal skills with a pleasing personality. Their best arena is in small group situations.

As with all temperaments, the Phlegmatic has a set of weaknesses. They are prone to lack decisiveness and enthusiasm, which is often masked by dry wit, aimed at the other 'uptight temperaments'. The worst scenario for the Phlegmatic is conflict, especially when confrontation is involved. The most glaring weakness is the Phlegmatic's lack of productivity. If not developed and encouraged, they can live their whole life without actually achieving anything or going anywhere.

The Sanguine Temperament – 'The Populars'

The Sanguine motto is 'Let's do it the fun way'. This desire is basic to the Sanguine temperament. Their emotional needs include attention, affection, approval and acceptance. They have high oral skills with storytelling that warms everyone's heart. Their best arena is among people, who all respond to the effervescent, optimistic personality of the Sanguine.

As with all temperaments, the Sanguine has a set of weaknesses. They are prone to exaggerate because of their 'sales pitch', can be gullible and naïve, and can be quickly impressed by other sales types. The most glaring weakness is the Sanguine's disorganisation. They don't necessarily intend to be disorganised, but there is just too much to crowd into their exciting life.

The Choleric Temperament – 'The Powerfuls'

The Choleric motto is 'Do it my way, now!' This desire is basic to the Choleric temperament. Their emotional needs include a sense of obedience, appreciation for accomplishments, and credit for ability. They possess the ability to take charge of anything instantly, and make correct, instant decisions. Their best arena is organising and coordinating people and events, and the bigger the better.

As with all temperaments, the Choleric has a set of weaknesses. They are prone to be too bossy and dominant. Sensitivity to people's feelings around them is not the focus, only the task at hand. As a result, the Choleric can become impatient and autocratic, especially if others won't do things their way.

The most glaring weakness is the Choleric's acidity in stressful situations. They simply turn up the ante, double their efforts and control, and blast away!

The Melancholy Temperament – 'The Perfects'

The Melancholy motto is 'Let's do it the right way'. This desire is basic to the Melancholy temperament. Their emotional needs include a sense of stability, space and silence. They desire sensitivity and support from those around them. They have high analytical skills with the ability to organise and set long-term goals. Their best arena is the area of compassion for the hurting.

As with all temperaments, the Melancholy has a set of

weaknesses. They are prone to become easily depressed as a result of their idealism and over focusing on the negatives, or things not turning out 'perfect'. The common response is to withdraw and give up.

The most glaring weakness is the Melancholy's fear of the unpredictable. They want a perfect, safe, and structured world. Their greatest dislike is people that sabotage this security through disorganisation, superficiality and compromised standards.

THE FOUR TEMPERAMENTS
Figure 1

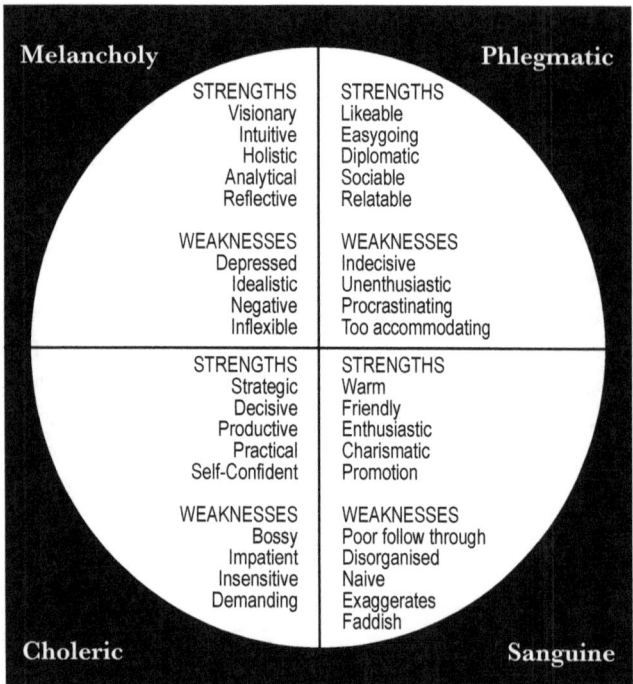

Melancholy	Phlegmatic
STRENGTHS Visionary Intuitive Holistic Analytical Reflective	STRENGTHS Likeable Easygoing Diplomatic Sociable Relatable
WEAKNESSES Depressed Idealistic Negative Inflexible	WEAKNESSES Indecisive Unenthusiastic Procrastinating Too accommodating
STRENGTHS Strategic Decisive Productive Practical Self-Confident	STRENGTHS Warm Friendly Enthusiastic Charismatic Promotion
WEAKNESSES Bossy Impatient Insensitive Demanding	WEAKNESSES Poor follow through Disorganised Naive Exaggerates Faddish
Choleric	Sanguine

Chapter Two

THE FOUR QUADRANTS

This model divides the levels of church leadership into four quadrants (fig. 2), using the four temperaments to illustrate the differing styles of leadership associated with each level of church life. Carl George's statistics in his book 'How to Break Growth Barriers' (p. 130) are quoted here.

It is important to note that we are making a distinction here between 'personality' and 'style'. Personality refers to an individual's temperament, whereas we refer to style as an individual's approach in leadership. For example, a phlegmatic personality does not assume competency in pastoral skills, just as a choleric personality does not assume competency in management skills.

Furthermore, these approaches can be learned and developed. For example, a Sanguine personality can develop the organisational skills of the Choleric style, and the choleric personality can develop the relational skills of the Phlegmatic style.

We have discovered that all leaders need to be aware of the human tendency to revert to our 'default setting'.

That is, our human preference to default to our natural personality or comfort zone and especially our natural strengths when feeling threatened. But this tendency can be unproductive in leadership. For example, an uncomfortable Choleric personality defaulting to a 'take control mode' in a small group setting would be inappropriate and unproductive. Just as a Phlegmatic personality defaulting to a 'let's just flow and be friends mode' in a Board meeting situation would also be inappropriate and unproductive. The key to effective leadership is to work out what style best suits the particular situation and adapt accordingly, rather than performing from a natural personality preference.

LEADERSHIP STYLES & LEVELS OF CHURCH
by Dr. Gordon Moore
Figure 2

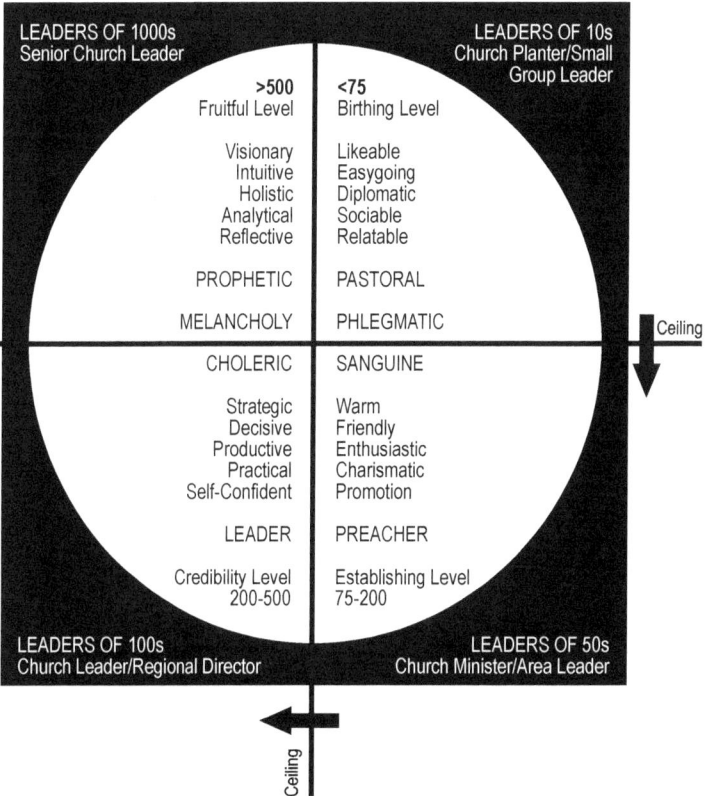

LEADERS OF 1000s Senior Church Leader		LEADERS OF 10s Church Planter/Small Group Leader
	>500 Fruitful Level	<75 Birthing Level
	Visionary Intuitive Holistic Analytical Reflective	Likeable Easygoing Diplomatic Sociable Relatable
	PROPHETIC	PASTORAL
	MELANCHOLY	PHLEGMATIC
	CHOLERIC	SANGUINE
	Strategic Decisive Productive Practical Self-Confident	Warm Friendly Enthusiastic Charismatic Promotion
	LEADER	PREACHER
	Credibility Level 200-500	Establishing Level 75-200
LEADERS OF 100s Church Leader/Regional Director		LEADERS OF 50s Church Minister/Area Leader

Ceiling

Ceiling

Quadrant 1: 'The Birthing Level'

The first quadrant is commonly known as the 'primary group' of up to 75 members. Fifty-one per cent (51%) of all churches operate within this quadrant[2]. It is called the primary group because these 'small group churches' consist of less than 75 members who are lead by one primary influencer, the pastor. It is also called the 'Birthing Level' because it is the stage of getting the church started.

The 'Phlegmatic Style' is used to best describe this level of leadership. That is, it is a level where the most effective style of leadership with less than 75 members is pastoral in nature, demonstrating a style of leadership that focuses on being:-
- sociable
- relatable
- easygoing
- diplomatic
- likeable

The First Quadrant

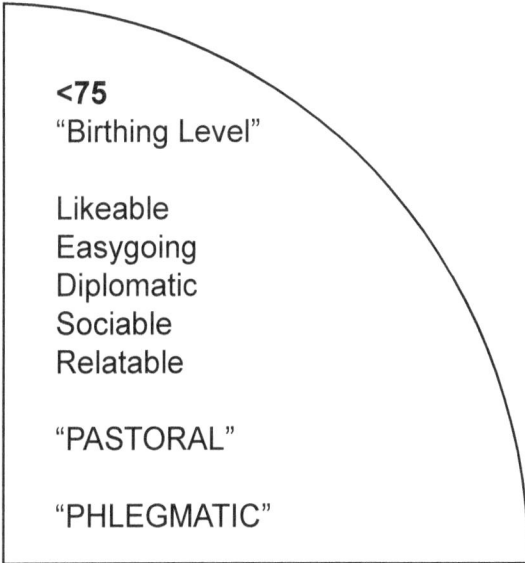

<75
"Birthing Level"

Likeable
Easygoing
Diplomatic
Sociable
Relatable

"PASTORAL"

"PHLEGMATIC"

Quadrant 2: 'The Establishing Level'

The second quadrant is the 'congregational group' of somewhere between 76 and 200 members. Thirty four per cent (34%) of all churches operate within this quadrant[3]. It is called the congregational group because these 'multiple small group churches' are led by one key leader or couple and a supporting team of small group leaders.

It is called the 'Establishing Level' because it is the stage where the church becomes a 'going concern'. In other words, it begins to feel like the church is going somewhere.

The 'Sanguine Style' is used to best describe this level of leadership. That is, it is a level where the most effective style of leadership with 76 to 200 members is ministerial in nature, demonstrating a style of leadership that focuses on being:-

- charismatic
- enthusiastic
- free
- warm and friendly
- promotion centred

The Second Quadrant

"SANGUINE"

Warm
Friendly
Enthusiastic
Charismatic
Promotion

"PREACHER"

"Establishing Level"
75-200

Quadrant 3: 'The Credibility Level'

The third quadrant is the 'non-congregational group' of somewhere between 201 and 500 members. Twelve point six per cent (12.6%) of all churches operate within this quadrant[4]. It is called the 'non-congregational group' because such churches break out of a small church mentality through the initiatives of the senior leader who moves from a minister to a manager.

This would be the greatest transition for leaders and churches to make, as most of the Australian population are of Phlegmatic/Sanguine personality types. These types are summed up in the Australian ideals of 'sticking with your mates' and 'she'll be right, mate'.

We term this level the 'Credibility Level' because it is the stage where the church can perform most of its activities with credibility.

The Choleric Style is used to best describe this level of leadership. It is a level in which the most effective style of leadership with 201 to 500 members is managerial in nature, demonstrating a style of leadership that focuses on being:-

-   strategic
-   decisive
-   productive
-   practical
-   confrontational

The Third Quadrant

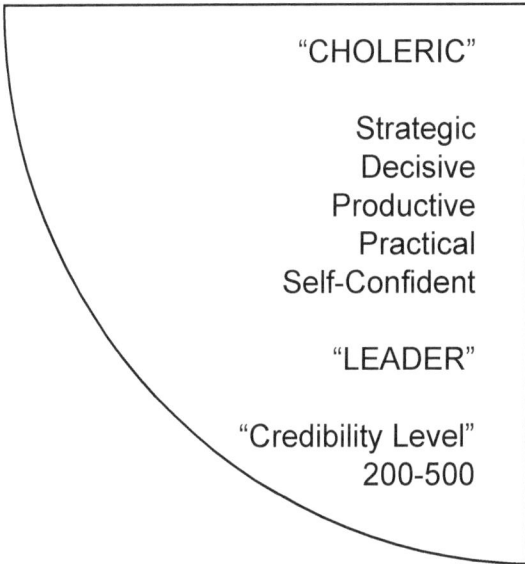

"CHOLERIC"

Strategic
Decisive
Productive
Practical
Self-Confident

"LEADER"

"Credibility Level"
200-500

Quadrant 4: 'The Fruitful Level'

The fourth quadrant is the 'multi-congregational group' of over 500 members. One point nine per cent (1.9%) of all churches operate within this quadrant[5]. It is called the 'multi-congregational group' because such churches have transitioned through the initiatives of the senior leader who has moved from a manager to a leader. Very few churches make this transition. The leaders of such churches have delegated the management of ministry in the church to others, who are now functioning in a choleric style, who in turn have delegated the ministry of the church to others, who are functioning in the Sanguine and Phlegmatic styles. It is called the 'Fruitful Level' because it is the stage where the full potential of the church begins to be realised.

The 'Melancholy Style' is used to best describe this level of leadership. It is a level where the most effective style of leadership with over 500 members is leadership in nature, demonstrating a style of leadership that focuses on being:-

-    visionary
-    analytical
-    intuitive
-    holistic
-    reflective

The Fourth Quadrant

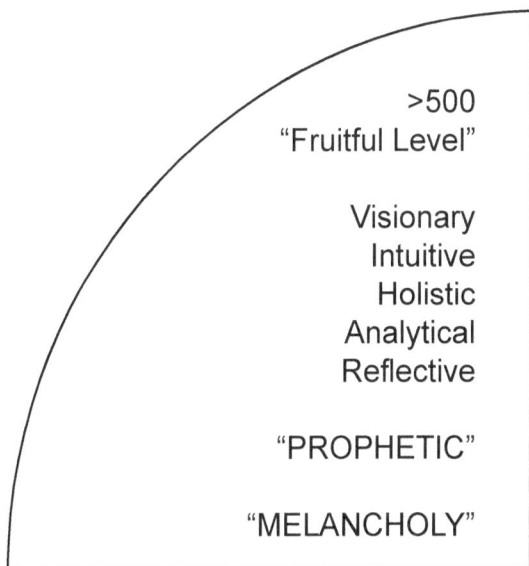

>500
"Fruitful Level"

Visionary
Intuitive
Holistic
Analytical
Reflective

"PROPHETIC"

"MELANCHOLY"

KEY COMPETENCIES

The Leadership Styles Key Competencies

Each style of leadership contains key competencies that make them effective at their particular level of leadership.

Quadrant 1: The Phlegmatic Style
(Small Groups < 75)

<u>Small Group Skills</u>
The Phlegmatic style is highly skilled in small group dynamics. This style displays high levels of competency as a '**small group builder**'.

<u>Relational Connection</u>
The ability of the Phlegmatic style to form one on one relationships that last comes to the fore. The ability to include others in close relationships is the key competency that enables this style to form a small group.

<u>'The Doer'</u>
The Phlegmatic style is the 'hands on' practical style of leadership that gets other involved through doing it

together. In other words, others help this style of leader do things.

Relaxed and Non-confrontational

The easy going, diplomatic style of this kind of leader makes it easy for others to be drawn into the group. There are no demands placed on others other than to 'hang and do stuff together', that is, to form close relationships.

Quadrant 2: The Sanguine Style
(Congregations 76 – 200)

Multiple Small Group Skills

The Sanguine style is highly skilled in multiple small groups, which results in '**congregation building**'.

Inspiring Togetherness

The Sanguine style possesses competence in oral skills, both personal and public, that inspires people to work together as a congregation.

'The Gluer'

The convincing warmth of the Sanguine style makes people feel they belong, that is, they 'stick' because of the charisma and warmth of the leader.

Quadrant 3: The Choleric Style
(Non-congregations 201 – 500)

Strategic Management Skills

The Choleric style is highly skilled in strategic management that results in '**non-congregational building**', that is, the ability to move the congregational group away from 'relational fixation' into kingdom purposes. That which builds the congregation from the primary group, that is, a strong sense of belonging to the leader and each other, becomes the barrier to growth and development at this level. For growth to occur and be maintained, the congregation must move away from merely existing 'for each other' and find a path towards fulfilling a great purpose and meaning for their existence.

Facilitator of Others

The Choleric style possesses a high degree of strategic skills, both personal and public, that recognises the strengths and potential in others. This style is able to facilitate people into productivity for kingdom purposes.

'The Organiser'

The success of the Choleric style lies in the ability to produce results through organising others effectively and not merely feeling good about belonging.

'The Confronter'

The confidence and robustness of the Choleric style enables an adjusting of lacks in others and blockages to progress without fear of the consequences. This style is unlike the Phlegmatic and Sanguine styles, which place a high emphasis upon 'people consequences'. To the Choleric style, task fulfilment replaces individual preferences and the maintaining of popularity as the leader.

Quadrant 4: The Melancholy Style
(Multiple Congregations > 500)

Analytical Skills
The Melancholy style is **highly skilled in analysis** that results in the ability to measure the actual progress of the church and its various components more effectively.

The Visionary Leader
The Melancholy style possesses the ability to 'see what could be', hence the term, '**the dreamer**'. The major transition achieved by this style of leadership is to move from manager to leader and so shift the emphasis in the church from task orientation to vision fulfilment.

Intuitive Leadership
This style of leadership becomes more focused upon the 'spiritual climate' in the church rather than simply achieving the vision through a series of tasks or ministry activity. The leader begins to ask such questions as, 'Is this pleasing to God?', 'What is the resultant atmosphere?', and 'Where is all this taking us?'

Holistic Approach

The Melancholy style leads in a holistic manner, this is, the ability to bring synergy among the multiple groups and agendas of others at the same time. This is termed leading '**multiple congregations**' because every department in the church is a congregation in itself by virtue of their size.

KEY WEAKNESSES

The Leadership Styles Key Weaknesses

As in the personality theory, each leadership style has its own set of potential weaknesses that can work against the effectiveness of the leader and ultimately the viability of the church.

The Phlegmatic Style

A Limited Worldview

The Phlegmatic style is focused on the immediate world of personal connections and relationships, which can work against the leader being able to embrace and cope with a growing and demanding network of people as the church grows. This limited view sees ministry only in terms of the personal contribution and connections of the leader.

Personal Contact Guilt

The need to be in personal relationship with everyone in their world, or church, becomes the undoing of the Phlegmatic style when growth demands that others share the load of personal connection. A heightened sense of guilt for not 'personally caring' for each member of the church becomes the barrier to growth for this style of leader. This style of leader tends to become captive to the over valuing of the personal contact of the leader with members of the church – an impossibility in a large church.

Unable to Sell

The Phlegmatic style highly values reality and genuineness in relationships, but this becomes a liability when the leader is required to promote his cause and 'sell the benefits' to others for joining his church. "If they can't accept me as I am, then who needs them!" exclaims the frustrated Phlegmatic style leader. But the reality is that unless this style of leader begins to promote his cause, few will be inspired to join the small group.

Diplomacy Sabotages Leading

The strength of this style of leader is the ability to build lasting relationships because of a non-threatening, diplomatic manner. However, this becomes a liability when the leader is viewed only as a friend, or 'one of the boys' by the members. They are therefore unable to address problems or strong people. It is difficult to facilitate change among equals.

This is a major break through key for the Birthing Level church. The leader must transition the church from being a primary group of friendships into a congregation with a leader who possesses a mandate to initiate change and growth.

The Sanguine Style

Susceptible to Fads

The Sanguine style is unable to resist the excitement and opportunity for the new and novel – a definite plus when the church is beginning. But once established, the congregational church can begin to haemorrhage at the never-ending pursuit of fads and the latest 'opportunities' available in Christendom. 'Variety is the spice of life', they say, but too much variety tires most people (Proverbs 25:16).

Uncompleted Projects

The prime focus of the Sanguine style is to launch, inspire and gather. This can lead to an over committing of resources on too many projects at once, which can result in not finishing the current ones. If this happens too often, a question of credibility can arise among the followers.

Won't Confront Others

The strong motivation to win people can become a negative for this style of leader when the same motivation becomes a barrier to confronting others about problems and obstacles that need solving for the health and progress of the church.

Won't Commit

In a world of ever increasing options, the Sanguine style leader can be all at sea when it comes to actually committing to a basic format for church life. In the beginnings of a new church, this is a vital component because the church is new, exciting and 'open and free'. People feel accepted and important. But as the church grows, the leader needs to concentrate on resources and activities, focusing on those opportunities that actually build the church. This however, is not easy for this style of leader, who can find themselves accused of not being consistent or reliable, and worst of all, being unpredictable – a liability in a growing church environment.

The Tendency to Over-Sell

The high oral skills of the Sanguine style, if not backed up by practical action, can be the undoing of this style of leader. Lack of substance, or results, can be the biggest danger for this style of leader who fails to develop competencies beyond verbal skills.

Can't Release Others

The need to be in the centre of the action is a needed trait when building the newly established congregation. However, this becomes a hindrance when the Sanguine style leader keeps wanting to be involved and be the central personality, and cannot release others to do the job and receive the credit.

The Choleric Style

Control Problems

The attribute that brings early success for the Choleric

style leader is the ability to take control and coordinate resources. However, once this has been achieved, the leader must authorise others to grow and contribute to the development of the organisation. But the Choleric style leader can have a tendency to maintain hands on control – a limitation for a growing church, which can result in the restriction of the much needed initiatives of others.

Impatient with Incompetence

If people fail to deliver anticipated results, the Choleric style leader can become impatient and take projects over. This can result in feelings of inadequacy in followers and a reluctance to be involved, which in turn adds to the frustration of the Choleric style leader.

Task Orientated

When the Choleric style leader becomes too focused on the tasks at hand, the organisation can begin to lack flow and feelings of appreciation. This style of leader can be perceived as 'non-relational', and even uncaring and lacking in compassion.

The Melancholy Style

Visionary Idealism

One of the significant problems facing the Melancholy style leader of a large church is the difficulty of both letting go all ministry and yet effectively keeping the vision doable for the average leader and members of the church. This can be achieved by keeping in touch with the leadership team, and ensuring that the vision does not become idealistic, and therefore perceived as undoable.

Loyalty/Disloyalty Fixation

The Melancholy style leader is motivated by the intrinsic nature of the church, not just the results on paper. In other words, this style of leader focuses on the engendering of the vision and core values of the church, and the leaders' and members' loyalty to them. If this 'loyalty' to the vision and core values is not being engendered, the Melancholy style leader can become concerned and feel that the church is being threatened by disloyalty. This is a key issue that must be settled for the large church to reach its full potential and fruitfulness.

Magnification of Negatives

The Melancholy style leader must not allow the analysis of 'the facts' to be magnified into paralysing negatives. It is important to deal with trends and indicators rather than the day-to-day statistics.

Chapter Five

KEY QUESTIONS

Leadership Styles Key Questions

A consideration of the kinds of questions that each style of leadership asks is helpful for several reasons. Firstly, these questions can help leaders understand what quadrant they are functioning in, and secondly, what kind of questions the leader needs to begin asking in order to initiate transition into the next level of leadership. For example, a youth leader operating a youth group of less than 75 people ought to be asking the Sanguine style questions, rather than remain stuck in the Phlegmatic style questions.

Phlegmatic Style Questions

1. "Which people **relate** to me?"
2. "What are these people's **needs**?"
3. "How can I **help** these people?"

Summary – the 'Who Question'
"What **people** do I relate to?"

Sanguine Style Questions

1. "How can I get these people to **join** me?"
2. "Are you **excited** about belonging to our church?"
3. "What are people's **feelings**?"

Summary – the 'What Question'
"What **program** am I promoting?"

Choleric Style Questions

1. "Who are the most **productive** people?"
2. "How can I **deploy** this person's gifts/skills to grow our church?"
3. "What are the **results**?"

Summary – the 'How Question'
"What **plan** are we following?"

Melancholy Style Questions

1. "Is every person contributing to the overall **vision**?"
2. "Are the core **values** and **culture** being engendered?"
3. "What are the **spiritual effects** of our activities?"

Summary – the 'Where Question'
"What **position** are we in?"

Chapter Six

APPLICATION:
OBSERVATIONS &
CONCLUSIONS

Observations & Conclusions

The application of this model over recent years has led to some helpful observations and conclusions:-

1. What is needed to start a church can often contribute to its demise. This is the situation where strengths become weaknesses.

2. Adopting a new style of leadership will initially cause reaction and loss before acceptance and growth.

3. Some leaders ultimately cannot or will not adopt a new style of leadership. We term this 'style lock' or 'default setting', which limits the effectiveness of the leader and the organisation.

Reasons for 'style lock'

1. **Sincerity**: a blind commitment to an out-dated and irrelevant culture and style of leadership. Sincere belief in certain philosophies and approaches to leadership can lock the leader into a certain style or approach to leadership that even though unproductive, cannot be changed.

2. **Reached leadership capacity**: all leaders have a capacity or ceiling, which will eventually be reached. It is my belief that each capacity is determined by the style of leadership of the relevant quadrant. For example, the Phlegmatic style has a maximum capacity of around 75 members. For growth to occur, the leader must adopt a new style of leadership.

3. **Don't see or know how**: many leaders have only operated within a certain style and context of leadership and therefore are unable to see or know how to transition. For example, a pastor who has only experienced small churches will tend to be unaware of the dynamics of growing a church beyond that level. Likewise, a leader who has only known the context of a large church can find great difficulty in planting, establishing, and leading a small church.

4. **Doctrinal and theological paradigms**: there are widespread belief systems abounding in Christendom that are counterproductive for the growth of the local church. For example, 'small is better', the 'unity of all churches', 'numbers are not Godly', and the 'servant leader' concepts are commonly held beliefs.

5. The **prevailing and existing culture of leadership** sabotages any transition for change and growth. This is especially so for the 'primary

group churches' (< 75) and 'congregational churches' (76 – 200) which consists of around 86% of churches.

6. The **leaders with the ability to adapt to and use** all four styles of leadership possess the greatest growth potential.

7. The **ability to focus on the key style** for any given stage of growth while not abandoning the others is vital to growth potential. For example, the following is a list of the leadership styles for matching scenarios:

    a. **Phlegmatic Style**
        i.   Small groups
        ii.   Visitation
        iii. Counselling
        iv.   New Christian follow-up
        v.   Conflict resolution (e.g. exiting and troubled members)
    b. **Sanguine Style**
        i.   Pulpit ministry
        ii.   New members classes
        iii. Vision casting settings
        iv.   Promotion of church/group/ministry to community
    c. **Choleric Style**
        i.   Board meetings
        ii.   Staff/volunteer facilitation and evaluation

   iii. Budget planning and review

   iv. Leading church through conflict/new ventures

   v. Pioneering new directions

d. Melancholy Style

   i. Vision casting meetings

   ii. Leadership training

   iii. Strategic planning

   iv. Spiritual tone

8. The need to **'come back the other way'** is vital for leaders. There are two examples of this. Firstly, a Choleric personality who begins pioneering a church needs to adopt a Phlegmatic style of leadership very quickly. I have observed successful, strong Choleric leaders from a large church setting, failing to grow a church plant simply because they continue to operate in a Choleric style. The key question to ask is, "What style of leadership should I adopt that best suits this situation?" Secondly, the larger a church becomes, the more aware the leader needs to be in recognising when and where to adopt a style that he no longer operates in by virtue of his position.

9. **Adopting a new style of leadership ought to be a process rather than an event.** My experience tends to indicate that time and communication are needed for the leader and the church to transition into a new style

of leadership. The best way to achieve this is through 'pre-wiring' the situation for the next stage of growth. For example:

    a. At < 75 begin to share **what the church/small group/ministry will look like** at 150-200 and what this will mean for you, your leaders and everyone.

    b. At 76 – 200 begin to introduce some **structures for growth**, including accountability and strategies. Gradually **become 'unavailable'** to the members of the church in terms of visitation and counselling. Delegate to others.

    c. At 201 – 500 begin to **authorise key leaders**, making other leaders accountable to them. Move the church into full accountability structures and budgets. Work on effective management.

    d. At 500+ begin to have **planned 'absences'** and so giving authority to other senior leaders. Move the church into a vision/values/culture/policy driven church.

10. My observation and experience shows me that the toughest quadrant to cross over is from the Sanguine to the Choleric quadrant. One reason could simply be that most leaders start out in

ministry because of a sincere love for people and the desire to help them; that is, they begin from a Phlegmatic/Sanguine style. They are indeed competent ministers for Christ. However, the Choleric style appears on the surface to be 'non-people focused', and some of the decisions that must be made for the health, growth and progress of the church or ministry seem to fly in the face of the 'ministry paradigm'. When a minister makes this transition, a leader is born!

11. There appears to be a clear distinction in leadership styles between the first two quadrants (Phlegmatic and Sanguine styles), and the last two quadrants (Choleric and Melancholy styles). The first two quadrants tend to be '**people focused ministry**', while the last two quadrants tend to be '**vision focused leadership**' (See Fig. 3).

In short, the first two styles seek to **build the believer** by **providing ministry to members**, whereas the second two styles seek to **build the church** by **coordinating the ministries of the members**.

ORIENTATIONS AND LEADERSHIP STYLES
Figure 3

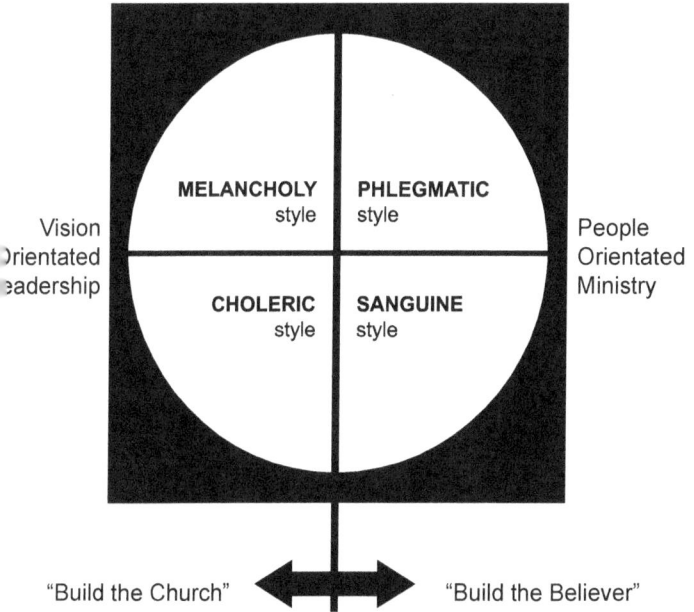

Vision Orientated Leadership

People Orientated Ministry

MELANCHOLY style

PHLEGMATIC style

CHOLERIC style

SANGUINE style

"Build the Church" ⟷ "Build the Believer"

THE LEAP FROM MINISTRY TO LEADERSHIP

The Leap from Ministry to Leadership

Figure 4, below compares the typical activities of 'Leadership and Ministry'. The leap from ministry to leadership is significant, and so are the results for the empowerment and growth of the church.

Figure 4

"Build Churches"	LEADERSHIP	MINISTRY	"Build People"
Leading and Managing	Purpose Values Direction Delegation Building the Team	Preaching Teaching Visiting Counselling Serving the Team	**Pastoring and Ministering**

Ministry focuses on the doing of the ministry whereas **leadership focuses on the empowerment of ministers.** In order to make the leap from ministry to leadership, the minister must cope with the feelings of guilt, 'I'm not doing anything', and shift towards, 'I'm equipping others to do'.

This paradigm change needs to happen at every level of the church. For example, a small group leader can remain a 'doer' with others helping him run the small group, or he can begin to empower others, multiply into groups, and become a supervisor over a network of small groups. The leap from ministry to leadership has occurred!

END NOTES & REFERENCES

End Notes

1. "Personalities in Power", Florence Littauer, Hunting House, Lafayette, Louisiana, 1989.
2. "How to Break Growth Barriers", Carl F. George, Baker Book House, Grand Rapids, 1993, page 130.

References

1. "How to Break Growth Barriers", Carl F. George, Baker Book House, Grand Rapids, 1993.
2. "Understanding the Male Temperament", Tim LaHaye, Commission Press, Charlotte, N.C., 1977.
3. "Personalities in Power", Florence Littauer, Hunting House, Lafayette, Louisiana, 1989.

www.ingramcontent.com/pod-product-compliance
Lightning Source LLC
LaVergne TN
LVHW051201080426
835508LV00021B/2742